A Note from the Author

To all the visionaries who strive to revolutionise traditional industries, this book is dedicated. From the golden arches of McDonald's to the principles of the Kanban philosophy, the journey of transforming fast food into a streamlined and efficient process emerges. With gratitude to those who dare to challenge norms and embrace continuous improvement, this book celebrates the marriage of innovation and tradition, showcasing the remarkable story of McDonald's through the lens of Kanban. May this dedication inspire future pioneers to reimagine and revolutionise the ordinary into the extraordinary.

Introduction

The McDonald's ordering process, with its digital display screens and order status updates, may seem like a simple and convenient way to get your favourite fast food. However, this system also holds a deeper significance when viewed through the lens of the Kanban philosophy. Kanban, a lean management system, aims to improve efficiency, eliminate waste, and promote continuous improvement. By examining the parallels between McDonald's process and Kanban principles, we can appreciate how this seemingly mundane task aligns with a larger philosophy of effective workflow management. Let's explore how the digital display screens, order status updates, and virtual queues at McDonald's demonstrate the core principles of Kanban, making the customer experience smoother, more transparent, and ultimately more valuable.

The Author

Julian Cambridge was born in London, UK.

- M.Sc. Business Computing
- B.Sc. (Hons) Computing with Business

Julian founded Golden Agile Solutions to supply IT consultancy activities to clients.

- Accredited Kanban Trainer (AKT, KMP, TKP)
- Certified Scrum Professional (CSM, CSPO, A-CSM, A-CSPO, CSP-SM)
- ICAgile Authorized Instructor (Agile Fundamentals, Agile Product Ownership, Agile Testing, Business Agility)

McDonald's

The process at McDonald's starts with a customer walking into the restaurant and approaching the digital display screen. The customer can then browse the menu options displayed on the screen and make their selections by tapping on the corresponding buttons. After selecting their desired items, the customer proceeds to the payment process.

Once the payment is completed, the customer receives an order number. This order number serves as a unique identifier for the customer's order. Simultaneously, the order details are transmitted digitally to the kitchen staff. In the kitchen, staff members receive the order details on their digital devices, such as tablets or displays.

The staff can view various status updates associated with each order, including "Order Received," "Preparing," and "Please Collect." These status updates provide real-time information about the progress of each order. The preparing/please collect screen is located near the pickup counter, allowing the customer to identify when their order is ready for collection.

The benefits of this digital process are notable for both customers and staff. For customers, having a clear display of the order status provides transparency and eliminates uncertainty. They can easily track the progress of their order from the moment it is placed until it is ready for collection. This enhances the customer journey, reduces anxiety, and improves overall satisfaction.

For staff members, the digital system alleviates pressure by streamlining the communication process. They no longer need to rely solely on verbal communication or handwritten tickets to receive order details. The digital system enhances efficiency, reduces errors, and allows staff to focus on preparing orders promptly.

The virtual queue is another important benefit in this process. When the customer's order number is in the preparing status, they can stay informed about the progress of their order by checking the preparing/please collect screen. The virtual queue reduces the need for waiting in line, as customers can find a seat or engage in other activities while keeping track of their order's status. This enhances convenience and improves the overall experience.

In the previous process without digital screens displaying order status, customers had limited visibility into the progress of their orders. They often had to rely on estimations or ask staff for updates, which could be time-consuming and lead to dissatisfaction. Likewise, staff members had to manage multiple channels of communication, potentially causing confusion and delays. These factors could create frustration and negatively impact both customers and staff.

The introduction of digital screens showing the status of orders has been instrumental in improving customer satisfaction and enhancing the overall customer journey. With the increased transparency and convenience provided by the digital system, customers are more likely to have positive experiences and return to McDonald's in the future. The retention of staff is also positively influenced by this efficient process, as it reduces stress and improves productivity, leading to a more harmonious work environment.

In conclusion, the implementation of digital display screens displaying the status of orders at McDonald's has transformed the customer experience. This digital process benefits both customers and staff, providing transparency, convenience, and efficiency. By alleviating pressure from staff and enhancing the customer journey, McDonald's can increase customer satisfaction and retain staff in their restaurants, ultimately resulting in a positive impact on the business.

Kanban

The above process at McDonald's, with its digital display screens and order status updates, can be related to the Kanban philosophy. Kanban is a lean management system that aims to improve efficiency, eliminate waste, and promote continuous improvement. It is often associated with visualising workflows and using cues to trigger actions.

In the case of McDonald's, the digital display screens act as visual cues that provide real-time information about the progress of each order. This visualisation allows both customers and staff members to have a clear understanding of the status of orders. Customers can easily see the preparing/please collect status and know when their order is ready for pickup. Staff members can also see the order status updates on their digital devices in the kitchen.

This visual representation of the order status aligns with one of the core principles of Kanban, which is to make work visible. By displaying the order status, McDonald's creates transparency and improves communication between customers and staff. It eliminates the need for verbal updates or guessing games, reducing waste and uncertainty.

Moreover, the digital process at McDonald's helps establish a virtual queue, which is another aspect related to the Kanban philosophy. In Kanban, queues are used to manage the flow of work and prevent overloading. The virtual queue in this process allows customers to see their order progressing through the stages of preparation, ensuring a smooth flow of orders.

The digital display screens also facilitate the concept of continuous improvement in the Kanban philosophy. By tracking order status and collecting data on the time taken for each stage, McDonald's can analyse and optimise their processes. They can identify bottlenecks, allocate resources more efficiently, and make adjustments to enhance overall productivity.

In summary, the process at McDonald's with its digital display screens, order status updates, and virtual queue aligns with the principles of the Kanban philosophy. It visualises work, establishes queues, and promotes continuous improvement. By embracing these Kanban principles, McDonald's can enhance operational efficiency and deliver a more satisfying customer experience.

McDonald's Drive Thru

The drive-thru process at McDonald's, when considered with the principles of the Kanban philosophy, showcases a remarkable integration of efficiency, waste reduction, and continuous improvement.

When a customer enters the drive-thru lane, they are greeted with a digital display screen that visualises the available menu options. This immediate visualisation aligns with the Kanban principle of making work visible. Customers can easily make their choices and proceed with their order, eliminating the need for paper menus or verbal communication.

Once the order is placed, the customer progresses along the drive-thru queue, and their order status is displayed on the digital screens. This visual representation provides transparency, allowing both customers and staff members to track the progress of each order. By adopting this Kanban-inspired visual cue, McDonald's promotes clear communication and eliminates wasteful guesswork.

In the kitchen, staff members receive real-time updates on their digital devices, signalling the status of each order. This integration of technology helps optimise resource allocation and reduces bottlenecks, aligning with the Kanban principle of continuous improvement.

By analysing the data collected through the process, McDonald's can identify areas of improvement, refine their workflows, and enhance overall productivity.

The virtual queue established by the drive-thru process ensures a smooth flow of orders, preventing overloading and minimising wait times for customers. Through the integration of visual cues, real-time updates, and continuous improvement, McDonald's creates an efficient and streamlined drive-thru experience that aligns with the principles of Kanban.

By appreciating the drive-thru process at McDonald's through the lens of the Kanban philosophy, we recognise the remarkable synchronisation of efficiency and customer service. This integration empowers staff members to work more effectively, enables customers to have a clear understanding of their order status, and paves the way for continuous improvement in McDonald's operations.

McDonald's App

Ordering via the McDonald's app, when analysed through the principles of the Kanban philosophy, showcases a seamless and efficient process that embodies waste reduction, transparency, and continuous improvement.

Through the app, customers are presented with a digital display of the menu options, allowing them to easily make their selections. This immediate visualisation aligns with the Kanban principle of making work visible. By eliminating the need for traditional paper menus or in-person communication, McDonald's reduces waste and streamlines the ordering process.

Once the order is placed, customers receive real-time updates on the status of their order. This transparency empowers customers to track the progress of their meal preparation, aligning with the Kanban principle of visualising workflow. By providing customers with clear communication and order status updates, McDonald's enhances customer satisfaction and eliminates the need for guesswork.

In the kitchen, the staff members receive notifications and updates on their digital devices, indicating the order details and progress. This integration of technology facilitates efficient resource allocation and minimises potential bottlenecks, in line with the Kanban principle of continuous improvement. Through data analysis and feedback collected from the app ordering process, McDonald's can identify areas for improvement, refine their workflows, and optimise productivity further.

The app also facilitates a virtual queue system, ensuring a smooth flow of orders and reducing wait times for customers. By synchronising the app's order management with kitchen operations, the virtual queue minimises congestion, eliminating waste and enhancing the overall efficiency of the ordering process.

By embracing the Kanban philosophy, McDonald's app ordering process streamlines the customer experience while promoting waste reduction, transparency, and continuous improvement. Through the integration of digital menu displays, real-time order updates, and virtual queuing, McDonald's maximises operational efficiency and customer satisfaction.

In conclusion, the app ordering process at McDonald's exemplifies the successful application of the Kanban philosophy. By leveraging technology and visual cues while striving for continuous improvement, McDonald's creates a seamless and efficient ordering experience that enhances customer convenience and operational effectiveness.

Ordering via Third-Party Services

Ordering McDonald's through third-party delivery services such as Deliveroo or Uber Eats, when evaluated through the principles of the Kanban philosophy, highlights the integration of efficiency, transparency, and continuous improvement in the food delivery process.

When customers place an order through a third-party platform, they are provided with a digital interface that displays the available menu options. This immediate visualisation aligns with the Kanban principle of making work visible, enabling customers to easily select their desired items without the need for paper menus or direct communication.

Once the order is confirmed, the information is communicated to the restaurant and the delivery partner simultaneously. This integration of technology ensures a seamless flow of information and enables real-time updates on order status. Such transparency adheres to the Kanban principle of visualising workflow, allowing both customers and delivery partners to track the progress of the order and maintain clear communication throughout.

In the restaurant's kitchen, staff members receive the order details on their devices, prompting them to begin the preparation process. By leveraging digital technology, the Kanban-inspired process facilitates efficient resource allocation, minimising bottlenecks and ensuring timely order completion.

Simultaneously, the delivery partner receives real-time updates regarding the order's progress and pick-up timeline. This synchronisation enables effective coordination between the restaurant's operations and the delivery process, enhancing overall efficiency and aligning with the Kanban principle of continuous improvement.

By analysing data collected from third-party delivery orders, McDonald's can identify areas of improvement within their operations. This feedback loop assists in refining workflows, optimising resource allocation, and streamlining the delivery process further. Leveraging this Kanban-inspired continuous improvement mindset, McDonald's can enhance their service and provide a more efficient experience for both customers and delivery partners.

The third-party delivery platform also employs a virtual queue system, effectively managing the flow of orders and minimising wait times. By synchronising the order management process between the platform, the restaurant, and the delivery partner, McDonald's reduces congestion and potential delays, aligning with the Kanban principle of waste reduction.

In summary, ordering McDonald's through third-party delivery services showcases the successful application of the Kanban philosophy. With digital menus, real-time updates, efficient coordination, and a focus on continuous improvement, McDonald's ensures a seamless and transparent delivery experience. By embracing these principles, McDonald's optimises the ordering process, enhances customer satisfaction, and drives efficiency within their third-party delivery operations.

Order Turnaround-Time: Restaurant and Drive-Thru

The order turnaround time within a McDonald's restaurant and specifically at the drive-thru can be influenced by various factors, and the principles of the Kanban philosophy can help optimise efficiency and reduce wait times in these settings.

In the restaurant, Kanban principles can be applied to ensure a smooth workflow and minimise bottlenecks. When a customer places an order at the counter, the staff receives the request and immediately begins the preparation process. By visualising the order on a digital screen or printout, the Kanban principle of making work visible allows staff members to track and prioritise orders effectively.

Efficient resource allocation is another aspect influenced by Kanban. By using technology to monitor the inventory levels of ingredients, the restaurant can ensure timely order fulfilment without delays caused by supply shortages. This enables staff members to have the necessary resources at hand, reducing potential wait times for customers.

Furthermore, employing a continuous improvement mindset derived from Kanban principles enables McDonald's to analyse order data and customer feedback. By identifying patterns and areas for improvement, the restaurant can refine their operations, optimise processes, and ultimately reduce the turnaround time for orders.

In the drive-thru, Kanban principles are also relevant. As customers place their orders through an intercom system, the visualising workflow principle comes into play. Staff members receive orders on a digital display, allowing them to track and prioritise the preparation process.

Efficient coordination and communication are crucial in the drive-thru setting, and the Kanban philosophy supports these aspects. By synchronising the order information with the kitchen staff and maintaining clear communication, McDonald's minimises errors, enhances efficiency, and reduces wait times for customers.

Kanban-inspired practices can also optimise the drive-thru experience by continuously improving throughput. By analysing data on order volume and customer patterns, McDonald's can identify strategies to decrease wait times and maximise the speed of service in the drive-thru lane. This could include measures such as optimising staffing levels during peak hours, adjusting the layout of the drive-thru lanes, or implementing technology innovations to expedite the ordering process.

However, it is important to remember that external factors and unforeseen circumstances can still impact the order turnaround time in both the restaurant and the drive-thru. Factors such as order complexity, peak hours, and the number of staff members available can affect the overall speed of service.

In summary, the Kanban philosophy can be applied in both the restaurant and drive-thru settings to optimise order turnaround time. By visualising workflow, ensuring efficient resource allocation, promoting continuous improvement, and enhancing coordination and communication, McDonald's aims to minimise wait times and provide a faster and more satisfying experience for customers in these areas.

Order Turnaround-Time: McDonalds App and Third-Party Services

The order turnaround time for ordering McDonald's via the app or through third-party delivery services can vary based on several factors, but the principles of the Kanban philosophy play a crucial role in minimising wait times and enhancing efficiency.

When placing an order through the McDonald's app, customers benefit from a streamlined ordering process. The digital menu display allows for quick selection of items, reducing the time spent browsing through traditional paper menus. Additionally, the app provides real-time updates on the order status, enabling customers to track the progress of their meal preparation. This transparency ensures that customers are informed about any potential delays or changes, minimising uncertainty and reducing the perceived wait time.

The integration of the Kanban principles in the app ordering process, such as visualising workflow and continuous improvement, helps optimise the turnaround time. By analysing data and customer feedback, McDonald's can identify patterns and bottlenecks in their operations, allowing them to make adjustments and improve efficiency over time. This continuous improvement mindset ultimately contributes to faster order processing and reduced wait times for customers.

When ordering through third-party delivery services like Deliveroo or Uber Eats, the order turnaround time is influenced by additional factors. Once the order is placed on the platform, it is transmitted to both the restaurant and the delivery partner simultaneously. The restaurant then begins the preparation process, and the delivery partner is notified of the pick-up timeline.

The Kanban-inspired integration of technology ensures efficient communication and coordination between the restaurant and the delivery partner, minimising delays and optimising the turnaround time. By visualising the workflow and providing real-time updates, both the restaurant and the delivery partner can track the progress of the order and strategise accordingly to ensure its timely completion and delivery.

However, it is important to note that external factors like traffic conditions, order volume, and distance between the restaurant and the customer's location can impact the overall turnaround time. While McDonald's and the delivery partners strive to minimise these external factors, unforeseen circumstances may occasionally affect the delivery time.

In summary, leveraging the principles of the Kanban philosophy in both app ordering and third-party delivery services helps streamline the order process and improve turnaround time. By visualising workflow, promoting transparency, and continuously analysing and optimising operations, McDonald's aims to enhance efficiency, reduce wait times, and provide a faster and more seamless experience for customers.

Summary

In summary, the McDonald's ordering process with its digital display screens and order status updates reflects the principles of the Kanban philosophy. By visualising the order status, McDonald's promotes transparency, improves communication, and eliminates waste. The virtual queue enables a smooth flow of orders, while the continuous improvement aspect allows for optimisation of processes. This integration of Kanban principles enhances operational efficiency and provides customers with a satisfying experience.

Foundations of Scrum Agile
Education

£2.99

App Store

Google Play

Agile Development with DevOps

Agile Project Management: Navigating Pros and Cons of Scrum, Kanban and combining them

Communication Troubles of a Scrum Team

Disney's FastPass: A Queue Story

Introducing the Douglass Model for Agile Coaches

Kaizen: The Philosophy of Continuous Improvement for Business and Education

Mastering Software Quality Assurance: A Comprehensive Guide

McDonald's: A Kanban Story

Scrum: Unveiling the Agile Method

Testing SaaS: A Comprehensive Guide to Software Testing for Cloud-Based Applications

The Art of Lean: Production Systems and Marketing Strategies in the modern era

The Board: A day-to-day feel of life on a Kanban team

The Sprint: A day-to-day feel of life on a Scrum team

The Whole Game: Systems Thinking Approach to Invasion Sports